Jack Johnson

ANTHOLOGY

CONTENTS

This book is printed on recycled paper

This book was approved by Jack Johnson

Photo by Thomas Campbell

Arranged by John Nicholas

Cherry Lane Music Company
Director of Publications/Project Editor: Mark Phillips
Project Coordinator: Rebecca Skidmore

ISBN 978-1-60378-104-6

Visit our website at www.cherrylaneprint.com

All at Once

Words and Music by
Jack Johnson

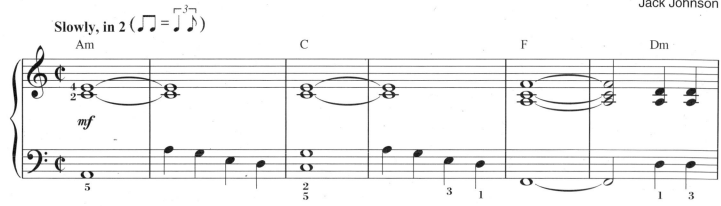

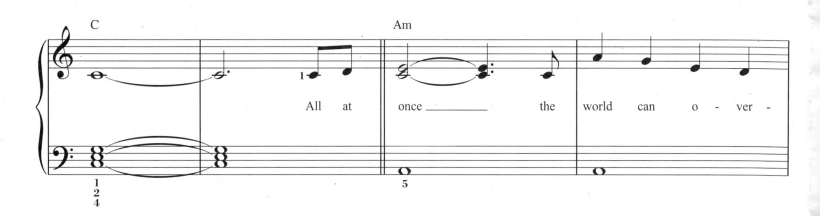

All at once ___ the world can o - ver -

whelm me. There's al - most noth - ing that you could tell me ___ that could ease my mind. _

___ Which way will you run? ___ When it's al - ways all a -

round you   and the   feel - ing lost and   found you a - gain, __   a

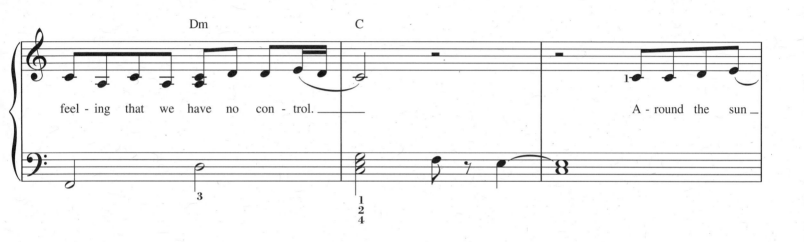

feel - ing that we have no con - trol. __   A - round the sun __

__ some __ say   it's gon - na be the new hell. __   Some say   it's

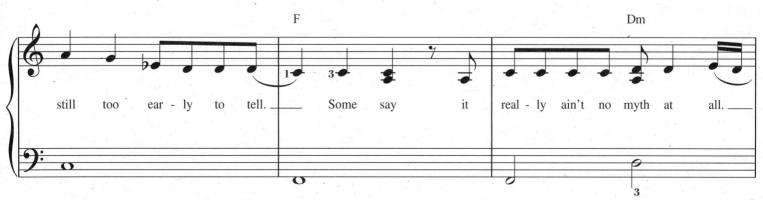

still too ear - ly to tell. __   Some say   it   real - ly ain't no myth at all. __

3

We keep ask - ing our - selves, are we real - ly

strong e - nough? There's so man - y things that we got

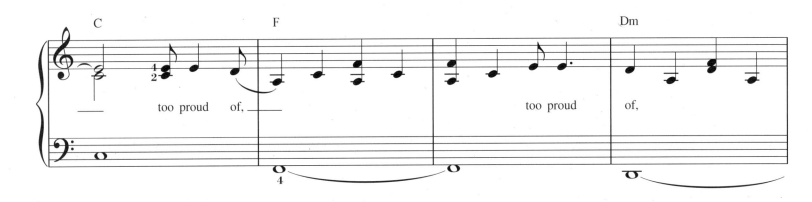

too proud of, too proud of,

too proud of. I want to

take the pre - con - ceived out from un - der - neath your feet. We could shake it off ___ and in - stead

we'll plant some seeds. We'll watch them as they grow and with each new beat ___ from your

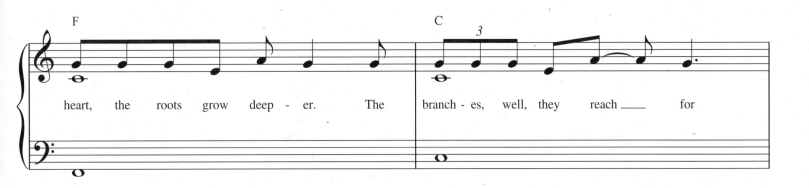

heart, the roots grow deep - er. The branch - es, well, they reach ___ for

what? No - bod - y real - ly knows. ___

But un - der - neath it all there's this heart ___ all a - lone. __

___ What a - bout ___ when it's

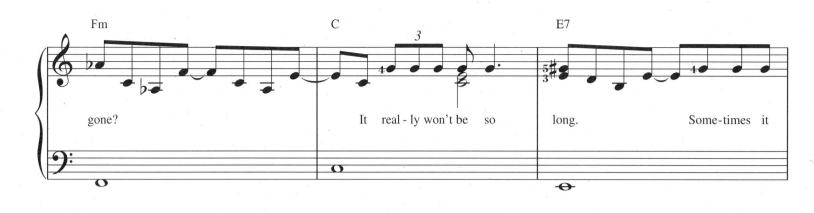

gone?   It real-ly won't be so long. Some-times it

feels like a heart __ is no place to be sing-ing from at all.

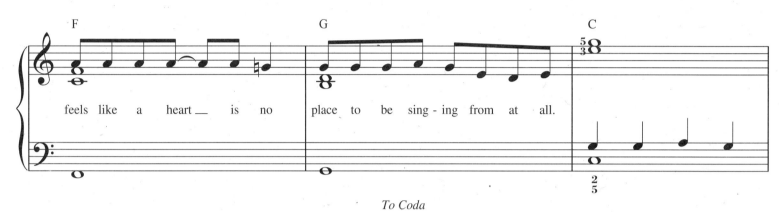

To Coda

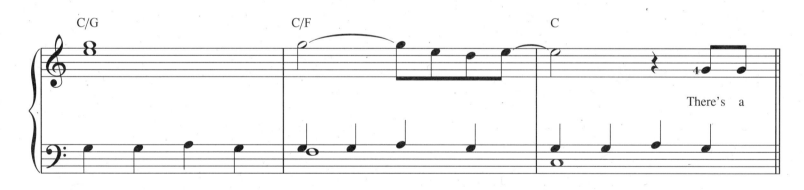

There's a

world we've nev - er seen; there's still hope be - tween the dreams. The weight of it all __ could blow a -

way with a breeze. But if you're wait-ing on the wind, don't for-get to breathe, 'cause as the

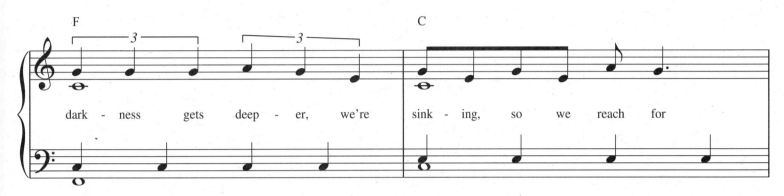

dark - ness gets deep - er, we're sink - ing, so we reach for

love. At least some-thing we can hold.____

But I'll reach to you from where time just can't

D.S. al Coda

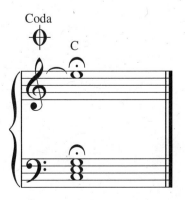

Coda

go.

7

Banana Pancakes

Words and Music by
Jack Johnson

Belle

Words and Music by
Jack Johnson

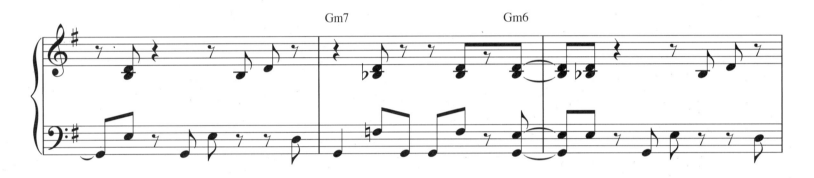

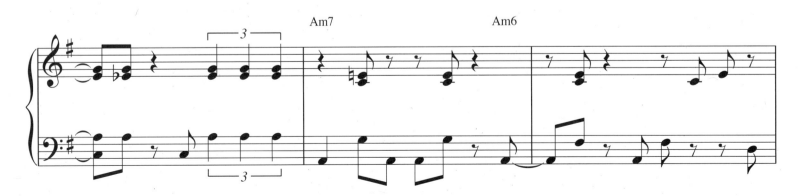

Oi, Li - en - da _____ Be - la che fa? _

Bo - ni - ta, _____

14

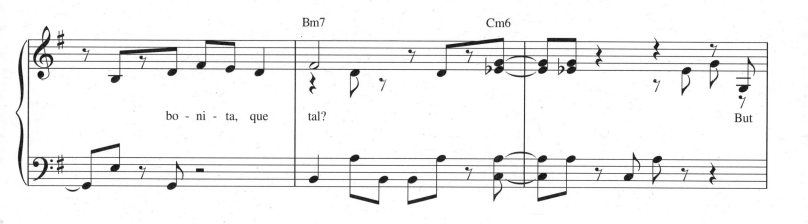

bo - ni - ta, que tal? But

belle, je ne com - prends _____ pas _____

_____ fran - çais. So you'll have to

speak to me some oth - er way.

Better Together

Words and Music by
Jack Johnson

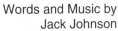

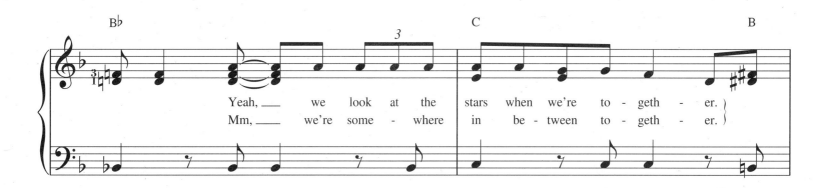

Yeah, ___ we look at the stars when we're to - geth - er.
Mm, ___ we're some - where in be - tween to - geth - er.

Well, ___ it's al - ways bet - ter when we're to - geth - er.

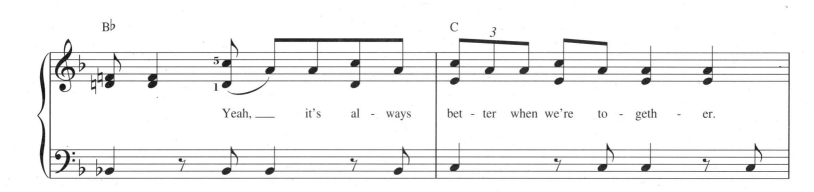

Yeah, ___ it's al - ways bet - ter when we're to - geth - er.

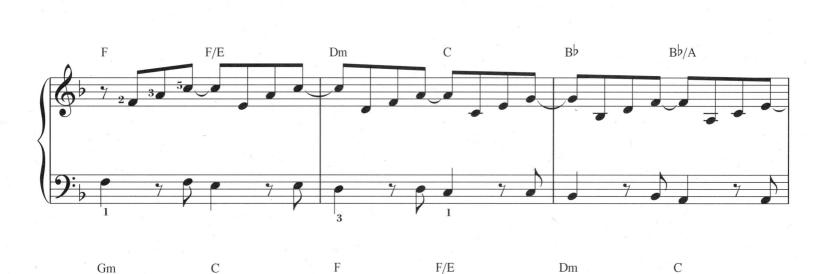

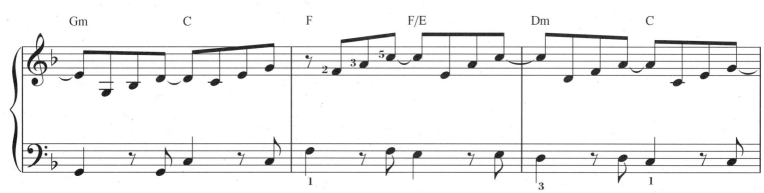

D.S. al Coda

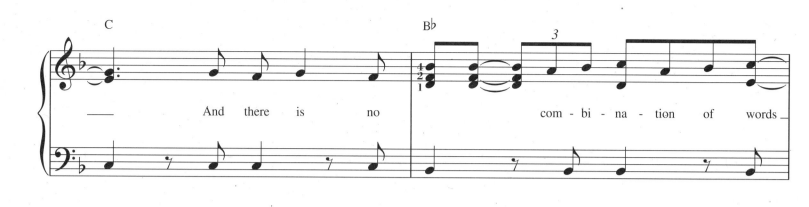

And there is no com-bi-na-tion of words

I could say, — but I will still tell you one thing: — We're bet-ter to-geth-er.

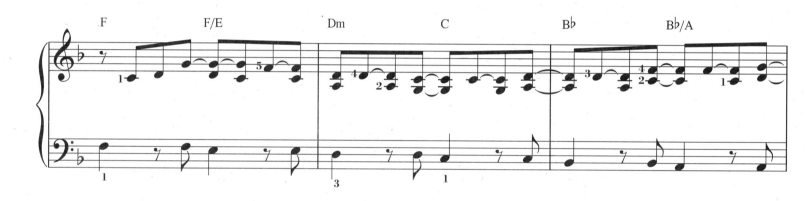

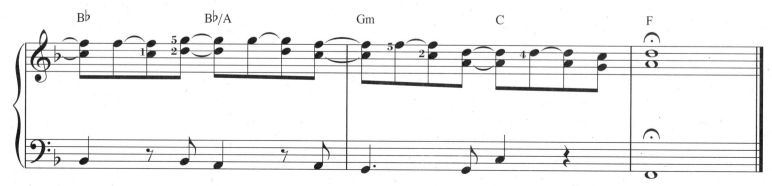

Breakdown

Words and Music by
Jack Johnson, Dan Nakamura
and Paul Huston

To Coda ⊕

Bubble Toes

Words and Music by
Jack Johnson

Moderately slow, in 2

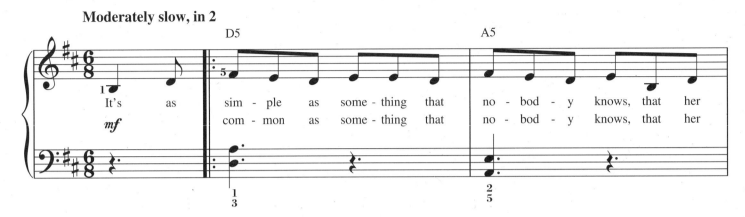

It's as sim - ple as some - thing that no - bod - y knows, that her
com - mon as some - thing that no - bod - y knows, that her

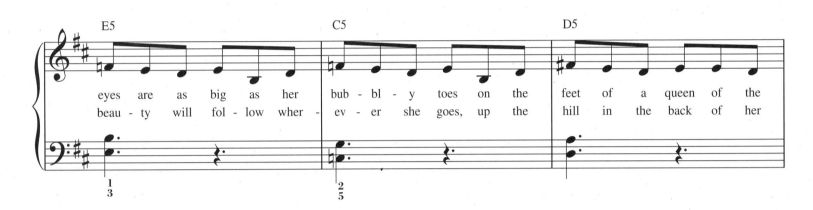

eyes are as big as her bub - bl - y toes on the feet of a queen of the
beau - ty will fol - low wher - ev - er she goes, up the hill in the back of her

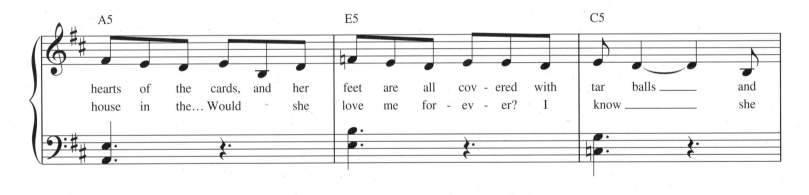

hearts of the cards, and her feet are all cov - ered with tar balls _____ and
house in the… Would she love me for - ev - er? I know _____ she

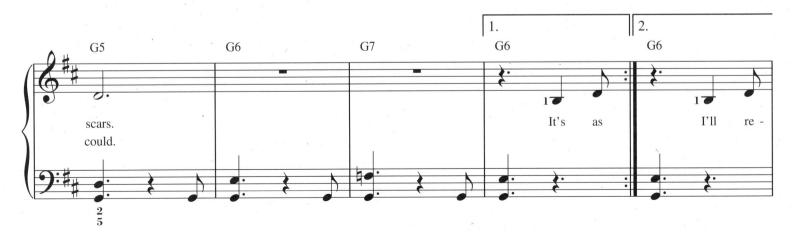

scars.
could.

It's as
I'll re -

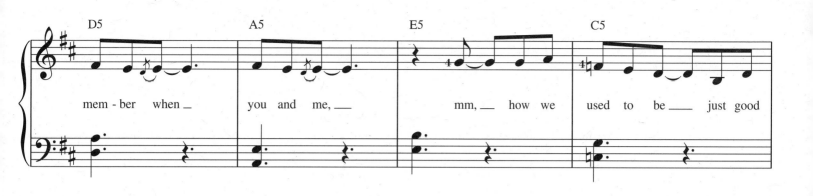

mem - ber when __ you and me, __ mm, __ how we used to be __ just good

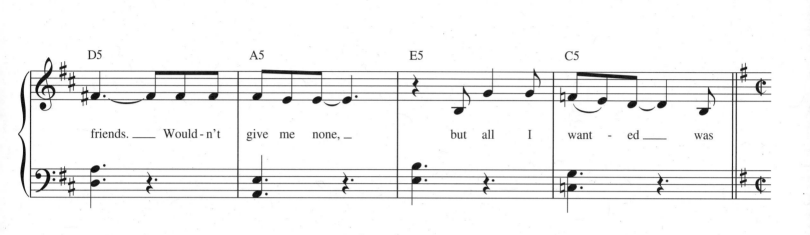

friends. __ Would - n't give me none, __ but all I want - ed __ was

Moderately, in 2

some.

She's got - ta whole lot - ta rea - sons. She can't think of a sin - gle one __ that can

justify ___ leav - ing. And he got none, ___ but he thinks ___ he got so man - y prob-

lems. Man, he got too much time ___ to waste. ___

His dreams are like ___ com - mer-

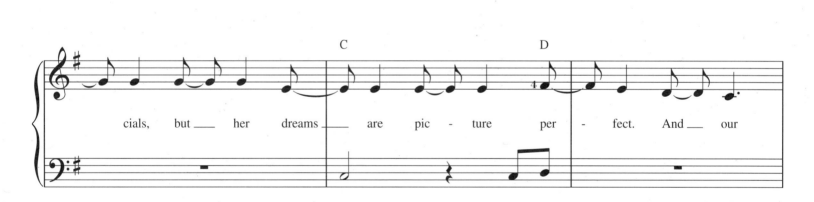

cials, but ___ her dreams ___ are pic - ture per - fect. And ___ our

dreams are so ___ re - lat - ed, though ___ they're ___ of - ten un - der - es-

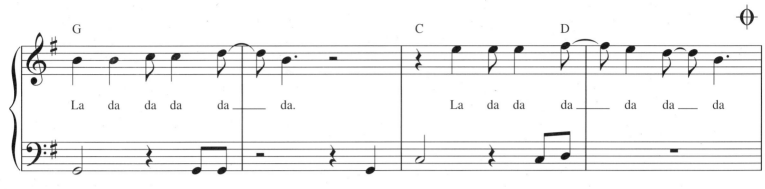

La da da da da da. La da da da da da da

da.

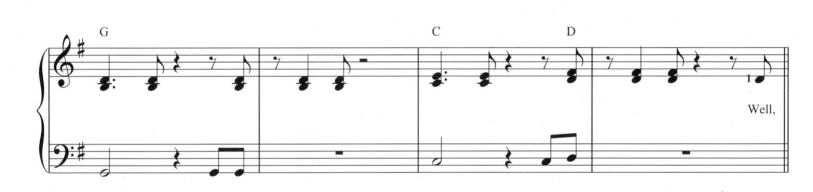

Well,

I was eat - ing lunch at the D. L. G. ___ when this lit - tle girl came ___ and she

sat next to me. Nev - er seen no - bod - y move the way she did. ___ Well, she

did and she does and she'll do it a - gain. When you move like a jel - ly - fish,

rhy - thm don't mean noth - ing. You go with the flow; you don't____ stop.

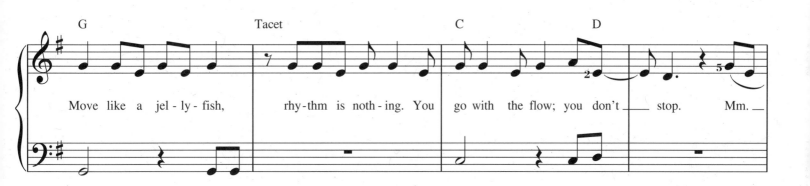

Move like a jel - ly - fish, rhy-thm is noth - ing. You go with the flow; you don't____ stop. Mm.____

D.S. al Coda I

It's as

Coda I

da.

If

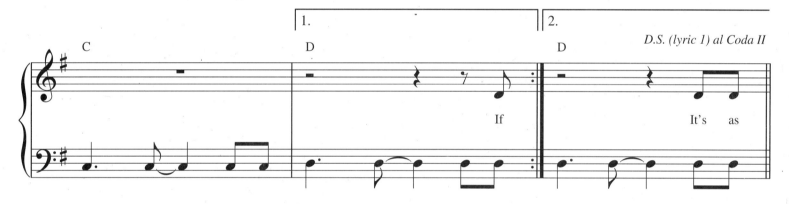

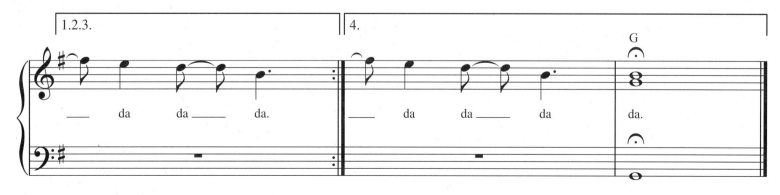

Constellations

Words and Music by
Jack Johnson

The light was leav-ing; in the west it was blue. __ The

chil - dren's laugh - ter __ sang, __ skip-ping just like the

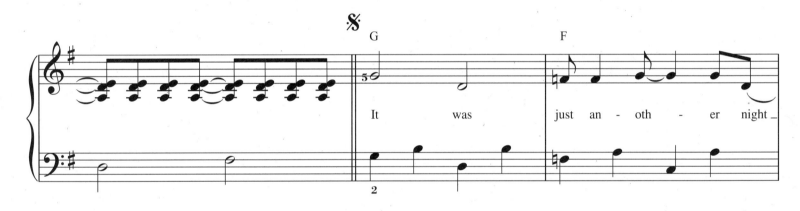

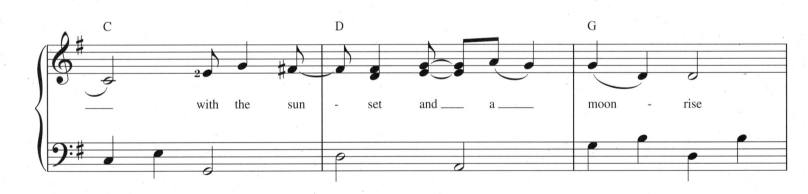

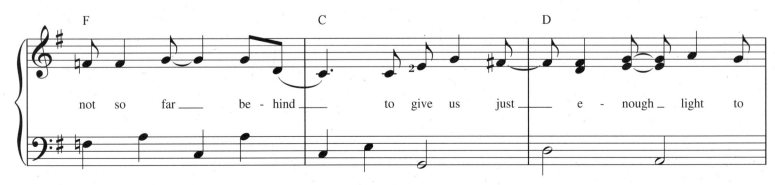

lay _____ down un - der - neath _____ the stars, _____ lis - ten to { Pa-
{ all _____

_____ pa's } trans - la - tions of _____ the sto - ries a - cross the sky. _____
the }

To Coda

_____ We drew our own _____ con - stel - la - tions. _____

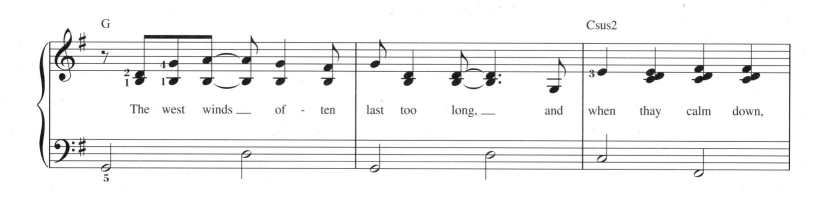

The west winds _ of - ten last too long, _ and when thay calm down,

noth - ing ev - er feels the same. _ Shel - tered un - der the Ka - ma - ni tree, _

wait - ing for the pass - ing _ rain. _ Clouds keep mov - ing to un -

cov - er the sea _ of stars a - bove us, chas - ing the day a - way _

_ to find the sto - ries that we some - times need. _ Lis - ten close e - nough, _

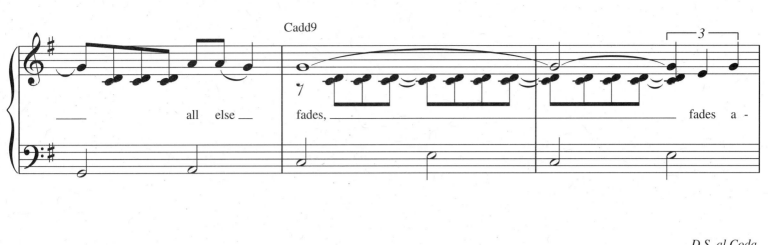

Cadd9

all else — fades, _____ fades a-

Dadd9

way. _____

D.S. al Coda

Coda

G   F   C

D   G   F

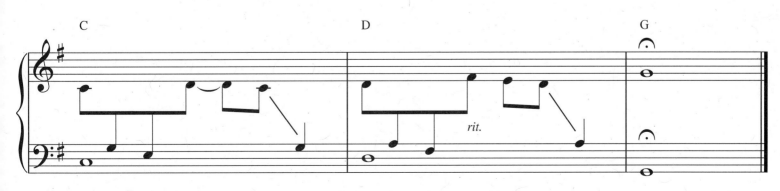

C   D   G

rit.

Cookie Jar

Words and Music by
Jack Johnson

Slowly, in 2

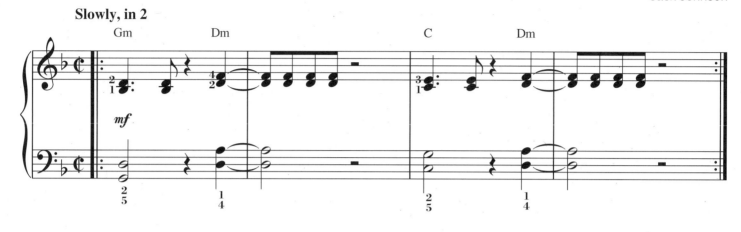

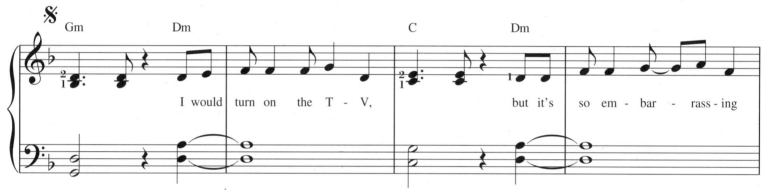

I would turn on the T - V, but it's so em - bar - rass - ing

to see all the oth - er peo - ple. { I don't Don't e - ven

know what they mean. And it was mag - ic at first,
know what they mean. And it was mag - ic at first,

To Coda

41

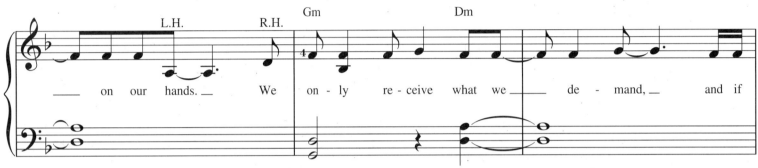

D.S. al Coda

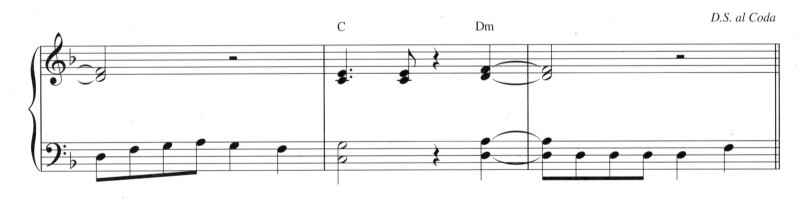

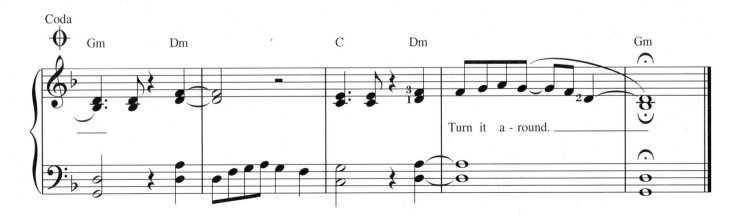

Drink the Water

Words and Music by
Jack Johnson

Drink the wa - ter, drink ___ it down. This time I know ___ I'm bound to

spit it back ___ up. I did - n't want ___ this

long e - nough, _____ I'll be home.

He's got de - lu - sions be - tween _____ his ears; _____ man, it takes

____ up too ___ much space. _____ And all that ten - sion be - tween

49

Fall Line

Words and Music by
Jack Johnson

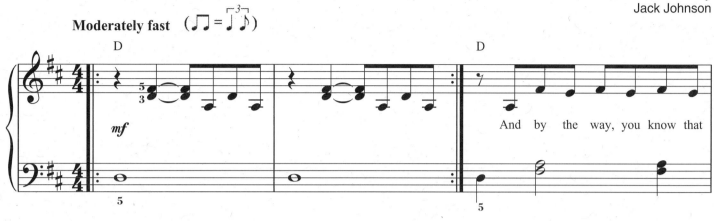

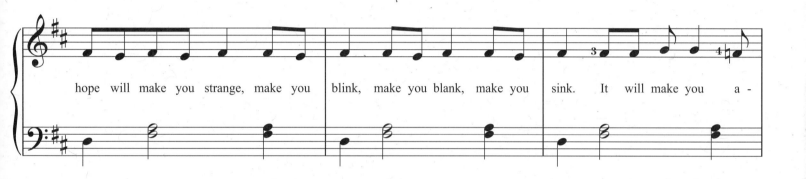

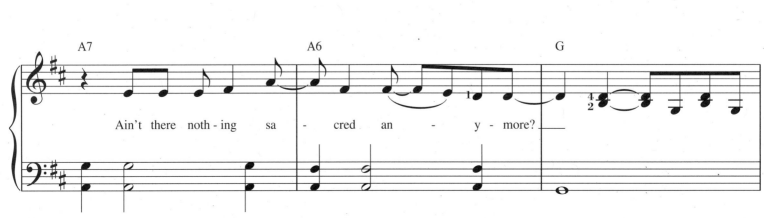

Op - ti - mis - tic hyp - o - crite that did - n't have the nerve to quit the

things that kept him want - ing more un - til he fi - n'lly reached the core. He

fell a - cross ___ the fall ___ line. ___ Ain't there noth - ing sa -

cred an - y - more? ___

Na na na ___ na na ___ na na na. ___

Flake

Words and Music by
Jack Johnson

I know she said it's al - right, ____ but you can make it up next time.

I know she knows it's not ____ right. ____

D.S. al Coda

I would-n't want to break 'em, nah, I would-n't want to break 'em.

May - be she'll help me to un - tie _____ this, but

un - til then, _____ well, I'm gon - na have to lie, _____ too.

It seems to me that "may - be," _____

it pret - ty much al - ways means _____ "no." So don't _____

59

Bb — tell — me; — you might just let — it go. —

C

F

C

F

F Hard - er than you try, ba - by, the fur - ther you'll fall, — e - ven — with

Bb

F all — the mon - ey in the whole wide world. —

C

Fortunate Fool

Words and Music by
Jack Johnson

63

F-Stop Blues

Words and Music by
Jack Johnson

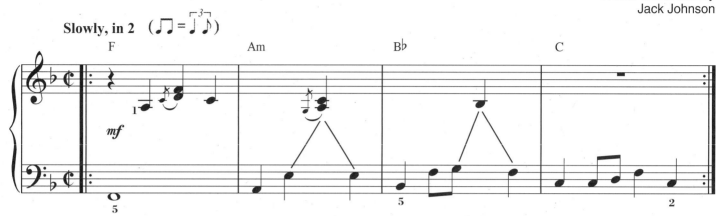

Her - mit crabs and cow - ry shells crush be - neath his feet ___ as he comes ___

___ towards you. ___ He's wav - ing at you. ___

Lift ___ him ___ up to see what you ___

can see.   He be - gins his fo - cus - ing. He's

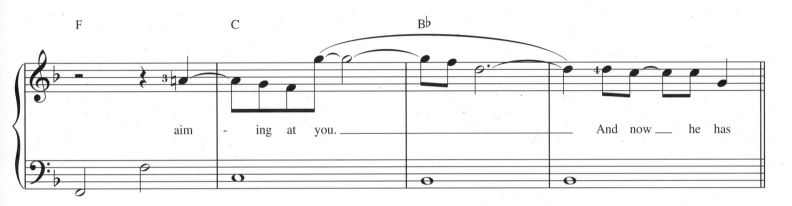

aim - ing at you. _____ And now _ he has

cut - a - ways from mem - o - ries and __ close - ups __ of an -

y - thing ___ that   he has seen or e - ven dreamed.

And now he's__ fin - ished fo - cus - ing. He's   i - mag - in - ing __

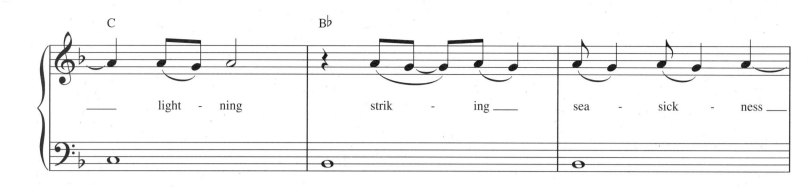

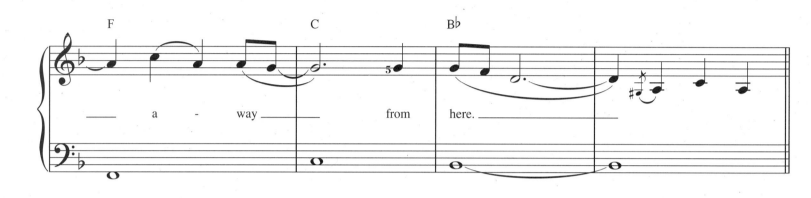

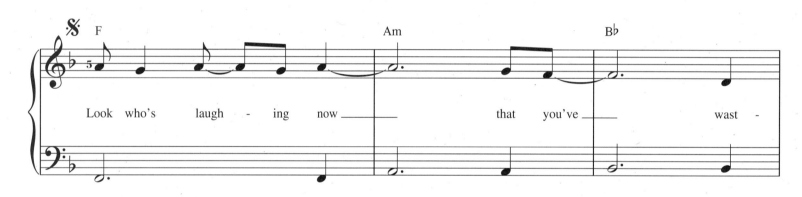

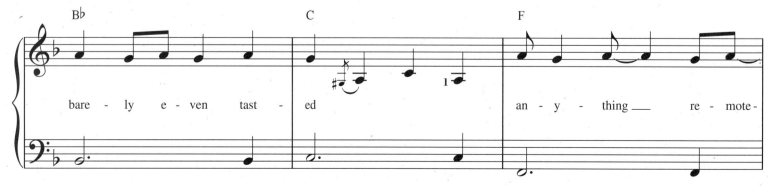

roots   to   ex - pose   them.   Quick - sand ___ steals   my   shoes.

Clouds   bring   the   f - stop   blues. _____

D.S. al Coda

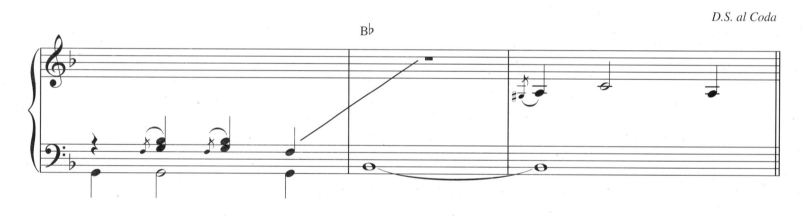

Coda

Repeat and fade

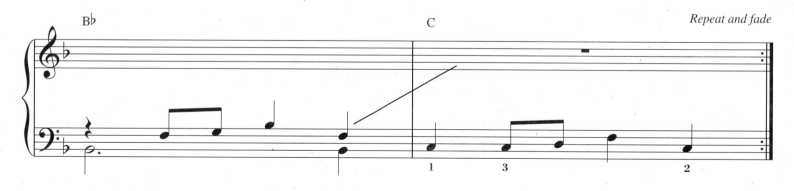

Go On

Words and Music by
Jack Johnson

In my rear view _____ I watch you _____ watch-ing the twi - light be - hind the tel - e - phone lines _____ with noth - ing to

D.S. al Coda

Good People

Words and Music by
Jack Johnson

Well, you win; ___ it's your show ___ now, so what's it gon - na be?

'Cause peo - ple ___ will tune in. ___ How man - y train wrecks do we need ___ to see ___

be - fore ____ we lose touch? ____ Oh, ____ and

we thought this ____ was low. ____ Well, it's bad, ____ get - tin' worse, ____

oh. Where'd all the good peo - ple go? ____

I've been chang - ing chan - nels; I don't ____

see them on the T - V shows.

Holes to Heaven

Words and Music by
Jack Johnson

There we were, __ stuck in __ } Port Blaire, __ where
mov - ing back __ north to __

boats break __ and chil - dren stare. __ There were so ___ man - y

few - er ques - tions when stars were still just the holes __ to

heav - en. Mm, mm. ___

And there were so ___ man - y few - er ques - tions

when   stars   were   still   just   the   holes ____ to   heav - en.

Mm. ____

87

Hope

Words and Music by
Jack Johnson and Zach Rogue

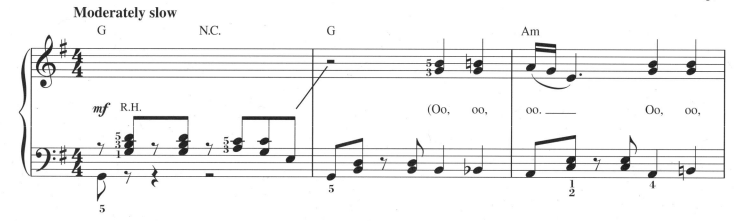

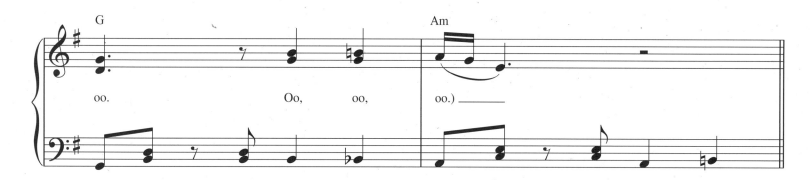

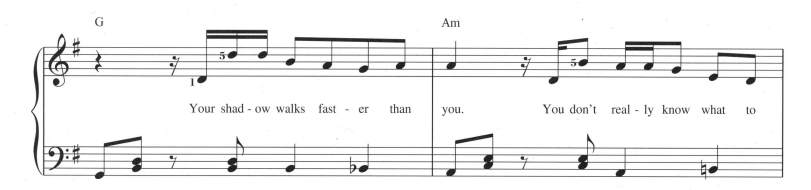

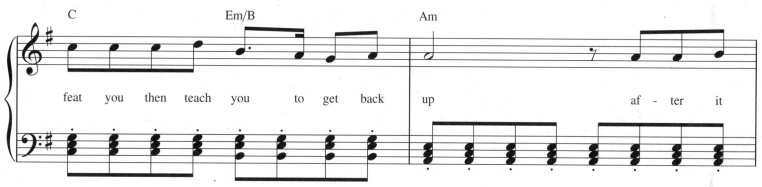

fu - sion, the frames the sun did burn at the end of a roll of de-

lu - sions, a ghost wait - ing its turn. Now __ I can see right

through... It's a warn - ing that no - bod - y heard. ____ It will

teach you to love what you're a - fraid of love, af - ter it
takes a - way all that you've learned to

takes a - way all that you've learned to love. But you don't
feat you then teach you to get back up. 'Cause

al - ways have to hold your head high - er than your

heart. You bet - ter hope you're not a - lone. You bet - ter hope you're not a -

lone. You bet - ter hope you're not a - lone. You bet - ter hope you're not a -

lone. You bet - ter hope you're not a - lone. You bet - ter hope you're not a -

To Coda

lone. You bet - ter hope you're not a - lone. You bet - ter be hop - ing you're not so...

Doo, doo, doo, _____ hope you're not a - lone. Mm, mm,

mm. _____ Your, your ech - o comes back out of tune. Now you can't quite get

used to it. Re - verb is just the room. The prob - lem is that there's no

truth to... It's fad - ing a - way too soon. Your shad - ow is on the

D.S. al Coda

move, and may - be you should be mov - ing, too. Be - fore it

The Horizon Has Been Defeated

Words and Music by
Jack Johnson

Coda II

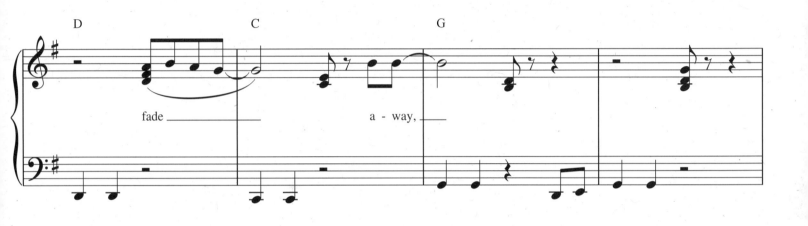

97

Inaudible Melodies

Word and Music by
Jack Johnson

Middle Man

Words and Music by
Jack Johnson

Moderately slow, in 2

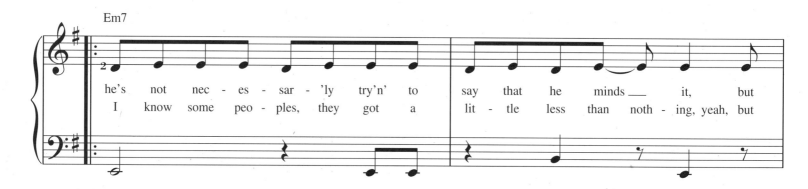

he's not nec-es-sar-'ly try'n' to say that he minds ___ it, but
I know some peo-ples, they got a lit-tle less than noth-ing, yeah, but

some-one plays e-vil tricks on that ___ kid. Yeah,
still find some to spare. ___

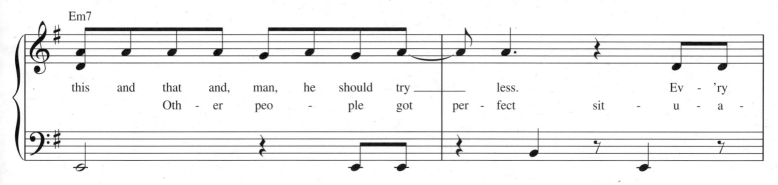

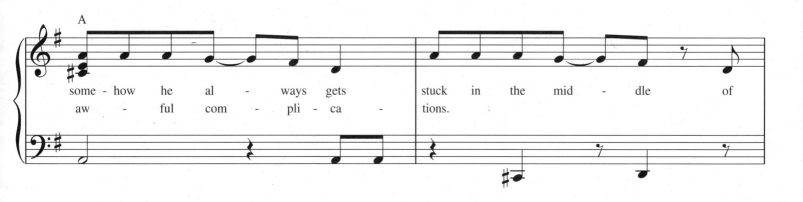

What an aw - ful thing ____ for you ____ to say. ____

What a ter - ri - ble thing ____ for you ____ to re - lay. ____

Well,

Mudfootball

(For Moe Lerner)

Word and Music by
Jack Johnson

Moderately, in 2

Sat - ur - day morn - ing and it's ____ time to go.
Sun - day morn - ing and it's ____ time to go. Been
Mon - day morn - ing and it's ____ time to go.

One day these could be the days, but who could have known? __
rain - ing all night so ev - 'ry - bod - y knows.
Wet trunks and school books and sand on my toes. __ Do

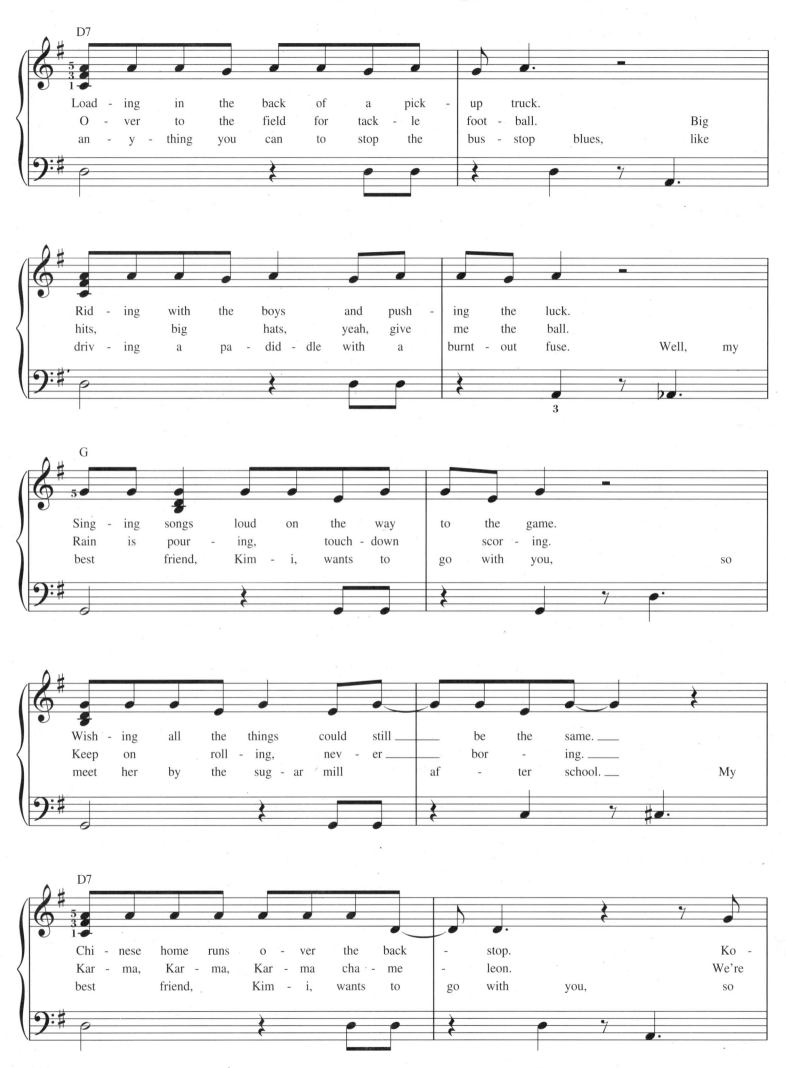

ku - a on the ball, and so - da pop. Well, _____

talk - ing kind - a fun - ny from he - li - um. _____ Well,

meet her by the sug - ar mill af - ter school. _____ Well,

Em7   Am7   C

we used _____ to laugh _____ a lot, _____ but on - ly be - cause _____

G   D7

_____ we thought _____ that ev - 'ry - thing good al - ways would _____ re -

To Coda

G   D7   G   D7

main.   Noth - ing's gon - na change; there's no _____

1.

G   D7   G

_____ need to _____ com - plain.

We used ___ to laugh ___ a lot, ___ but on - ly be - cause ___

we thought __ that ev - 'ry - thing good al - ways would, __

ev - 'ry - thing good al - ways would __ re - main. __

Mm. _____

Repeat and fade

Posters

Words and Music by
Jack Johnson

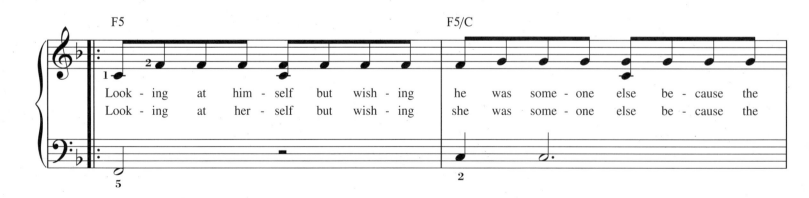

Look - ing at him - self but wish - ing he was some - one else be - cause the

Look - ing at her - self but wish - ing she was some - one else be - cause the

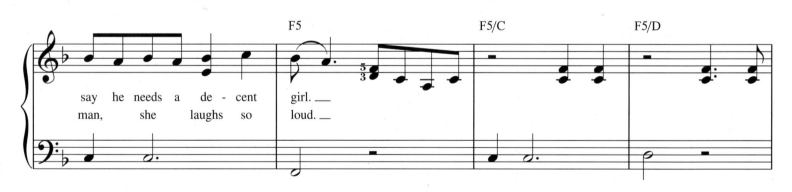

And if it ain't this, then it's that. As a mat-ter of

fact, she has-n't had ___ a day ___ to re - lax ___ since she's ___

lost her ___ a - bil - i - ty ___ to think clear - ly.

Well, I'm an

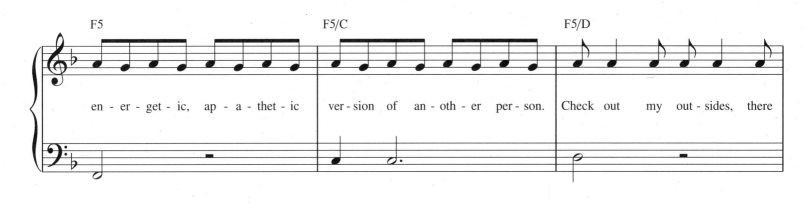

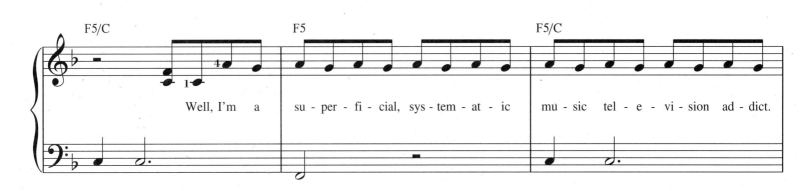

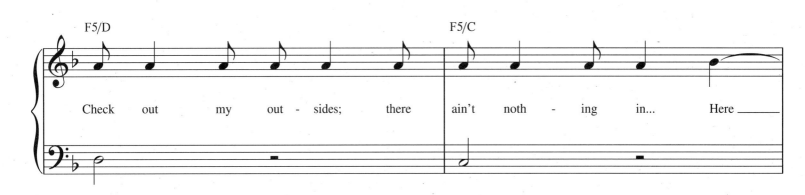

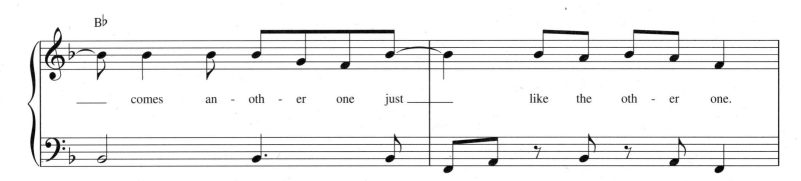

Looking at himself but wishing he was someone else because the

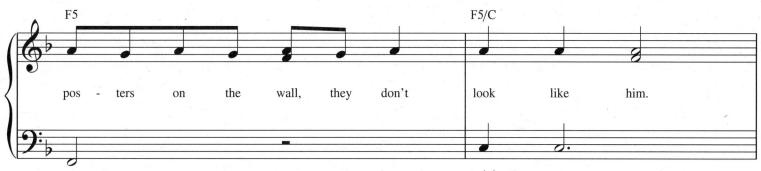

posters on the wall, they don't look like him.

Tie it up, he tucks it in, he pulls it back and gives a grin,

laughing at himself because he knows he ain't loved at

all. He knows he ain't loved at all. _____

Sitting, Waiting, Wishing

Words and Music by
Jack Johnson

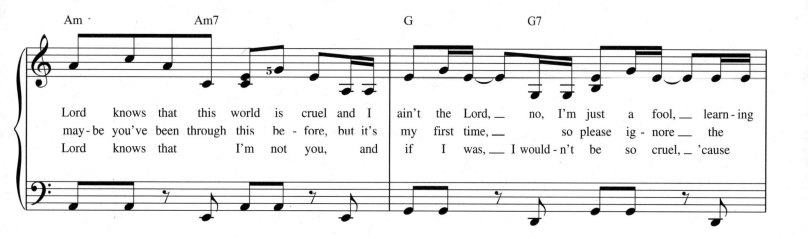

Lord   knows   that   this   world   is cruel and I   ain't the   Lord,   no, I'm just   a   fool, learn-ing
may-be you've been through this be - fore, but it's my   first time,   so please ig - nore the
Lord   knows that   I'm not you, and if   I was, I would - n't be   so cruel, 'cause

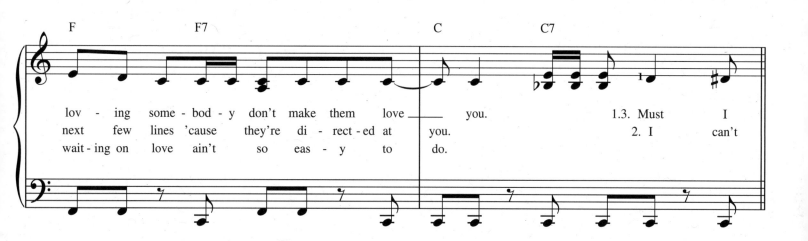

lov - ing some - bod - y don't make them love   you.   1.3. Must   I
next few   lines 'cause they're di - rect - ed at you.   2. I   can't
wait - ing on   love ain't so eas - y to   do.

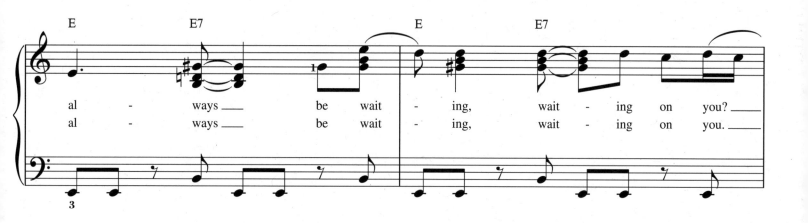

al -   ways   be wait - ing, wait - ing on you?
al -   ways   be wait - ing, wait - ing on you.

Must   I
I   can't

Staple It Together

Lyrics by
Jack Johnson

Music by
Jack Johnson and Merlo Podlewski

it bad weath-er. Sta-ple it to-geth-er and call ___ it bad weath-er. Mm,

mm. ___

Well, I ___ it bad weath-er. Mm,

mm. ___

Taylor

Words and Music by
Jack Johnson

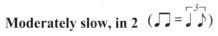

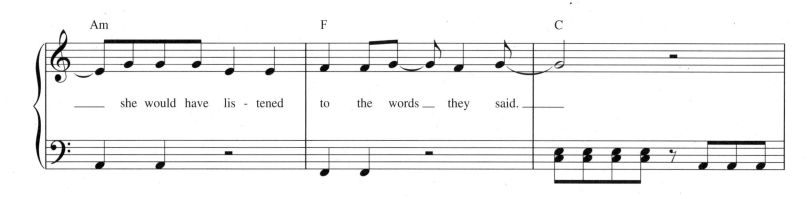

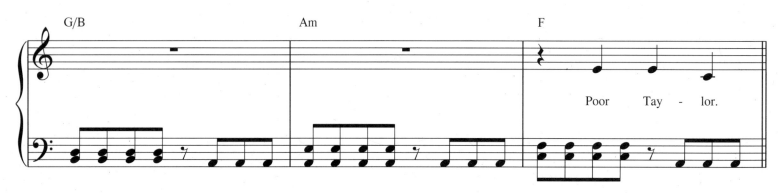

She } just wan - ders a - round, ____ un - af - fect - ed by ____

the win - ter winds, ____ yeah. And {she'll he'll} pre - tend ____ that

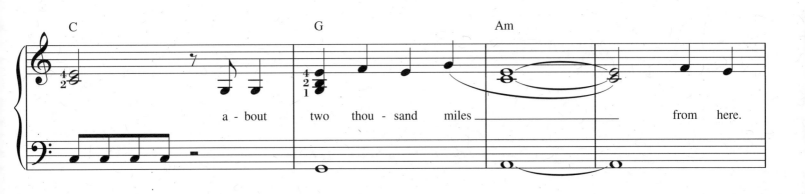

{she's he's} some - where else ____ so far and clear, ____

a - bout two thou - sand miles ____ from here.

to the man___ with the mon-ey in his pock-et, fly - ing in his rock-et, on -

ly stop-ping by on his way to a bet - ter world.___

If Tay-lor finds a bet - ter world,___

$(\sqcap = \sqcap^{3})$

then Tay - lor's gon - na run a - way.___

D.S.S. al Fine

Times Like These

Words and Music by
Jack Johnson

138

Traffic in the Sky

Words and Music by
Jack Johnson